on the plane

Carron Brown

Illustrated by Bee Johnson

Kane Miller
A DIVISION OF EDC PUBLISHING

An airport is busy with planes and people.

If you peer between the check-in desks,
through the terminal, and inside the planes,
you can see the people who work for the airlines.

Shine a flashlight behind the page
or hold it to the light to reveal pilots,
cabin crew, and plane parts and types.
Discover a world of great surprises.

People stand in a line at the check-in desk.

Can you see who is looking at the tickets?

"Next!"

Airline staff check the passports, tickets, and bags that will be placed in the bottom of the plane.

They make sure people are ready to travel.

After check-in, each passenger goes through security. Bags are X-rayed and people are scanned for dangerous objects.

What can you see on the X-ray?

The X-ray is quick and safe.

People pick up their bags
and go to the plane.

Zap!

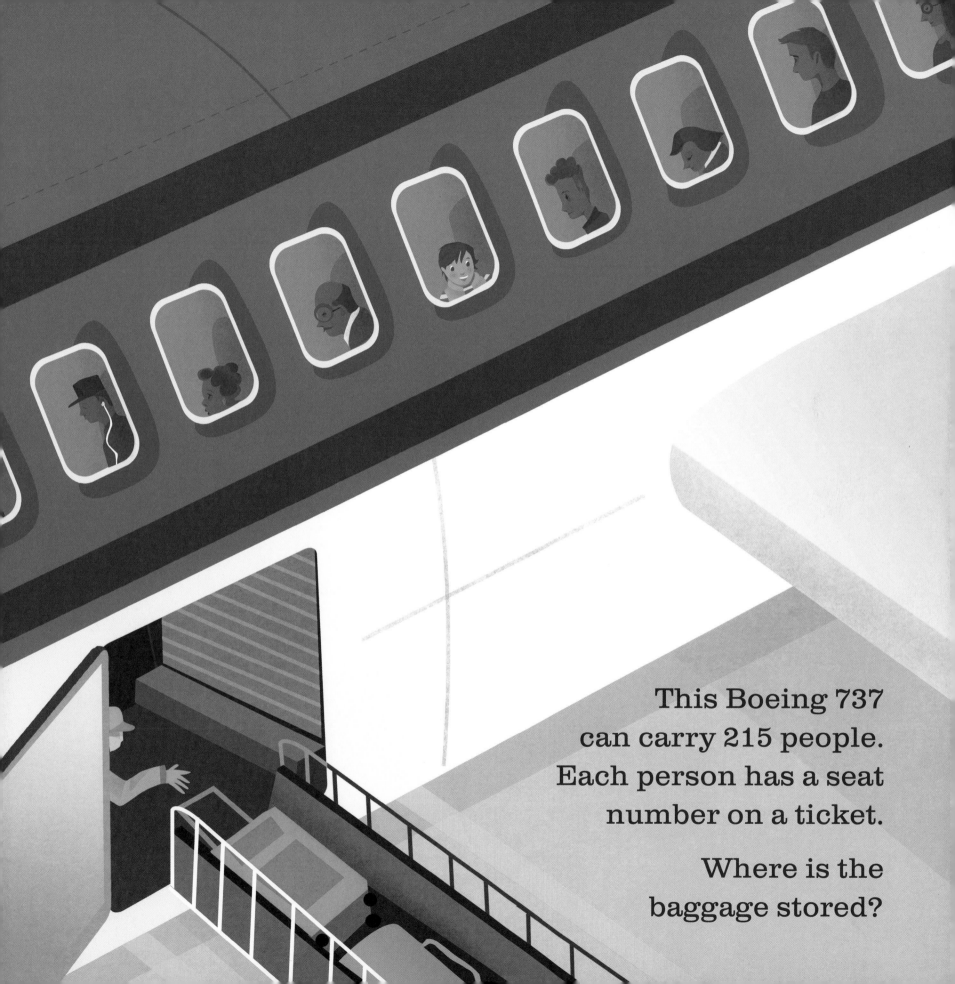

This Boeing 737 can carry 215 people. Each person has a seat number on a ticket.

Where is the baggage stored?

Click!

Hand baggage is put in
the overhead bins above the
seats. Large bags are loaded into
the hold at the bottom of the plane.

Chocks away!

The wheel chocks that stop the plane have to be taken away before the plane can move.

Can you see who is signaling?

Swish!

An airport marshaller waves
colored wands to guide
the pilot to the runway.

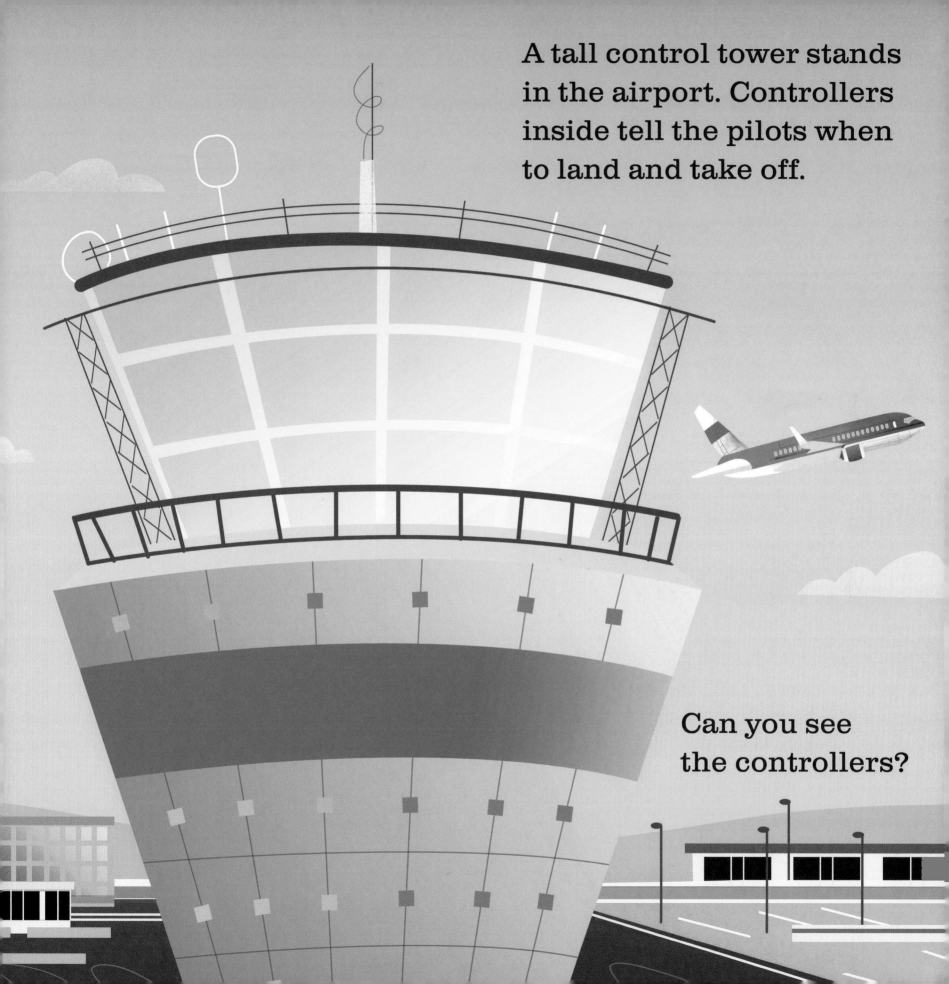

A tall control tower stands in the airport. Controllers inside tell the pilots when to land and take off.

Can you see the controllers?

"Cleared for takeoff!"

Controllers use radios to talk to
the pilots. Computer screens show
where the planes are in the sky.

The plane has two enormous engines, one on each wing.

How do they work?

Roar!

A huge, spinning fan inside each engine sucks in air.

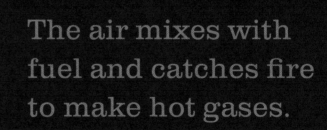

The air mixes with fuel and catches fire to make hot gases.

The gases shoot backward and push the plane forward.

Just before takeoff, a member of the cabin crew shows the passengers how to put on a life jacket.

Where are the passengers' life jackets?

There's a life jacket under every seat.

There are many planes in the sky. Air traffic controllers make sure they fly different routes.

Can you see any other planes?

Whirr!

Each plane has a signal that is picked up by the air traffic control radar.

Air traffic controllers make sure that the planes don't fly too close to each other.

The plane is flying above the clouds.

Can you see inside the cockpit?

Beep!

The pilot switches on the
autopilot and a computer
flies the plane.

The pilot and copilot check
the route and stay in touch
with the air traffic controllers.

The plane has special
parts to help it turn.

Can you see them?

The tail and wings have parts
that move to turn the plane.
The rudder on the tail goes
from side to side.

Swoosh!

One of the cabin crew comes around with a service cart.

Can you see what's inside?

Crunch!

There are lots of different
types of drinks and yummy
snacks in the service cart.

Slurp!

People do all sorts of things on a plane.

Can you see what some of them are doing?

On large planes, there are
screens on the backs of
the seats.

People watch cartoons and
movies, and can play games.

As the plane nears the end of its trip,
it flies down toward the runway.

Where are its wheels?

The plane's wheels tuck underneath the plane after takeoff. Now they move down so the plane can land.

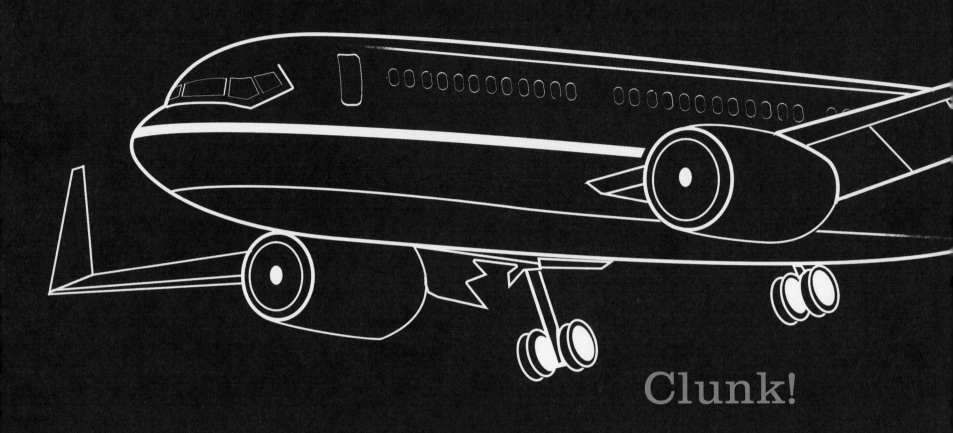

Clunk!

After landing, airport staff start unloading the bags.
How do people get from the plane into the airport?

A special corridor on wheels connects the plane to the building.

It is time to find the bags.
They are loaded on a truck
from the plane and driven
to the baggage area.

2

Where are
the bags now?

The bags travel down
a moving carousel
from the baggage truck
into the building.

People find and
collect their luggage.

Swish!

Bump!

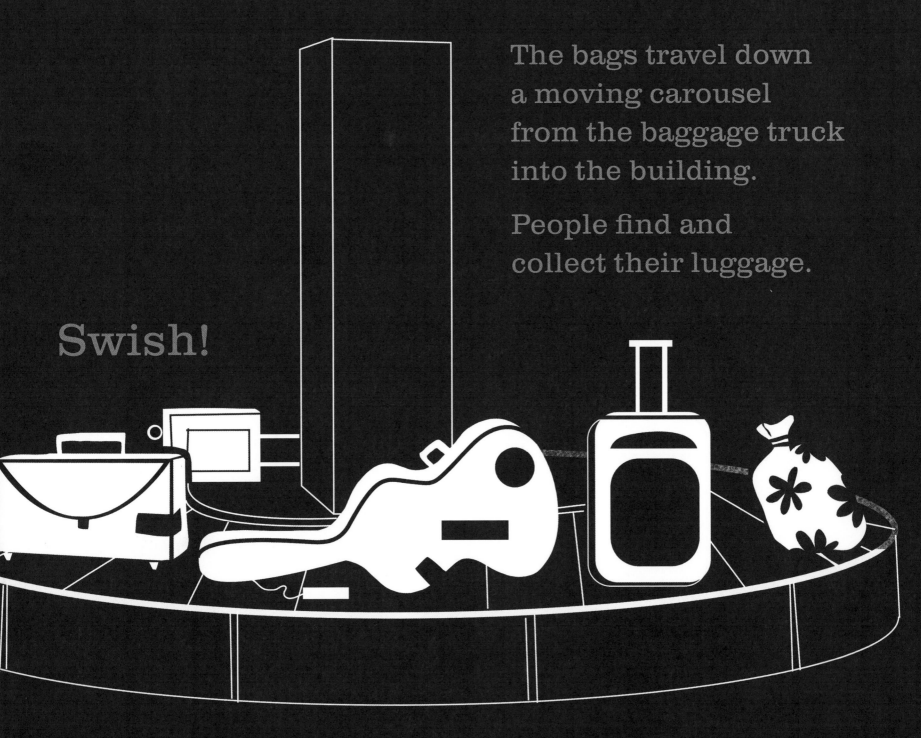

While the passengers were getting their bags, our plane was cleaned and given fuel.

From inside the airport, we can see our plane take off again to fly to another destination.

There's more...

There is a lot to spot in a plane and at an airport. Here are some people and objects you have read about in this book.

Pilot and copilot The pilot is the person who is in charge of flying the plane and making sure the plane and passengers are safe. The pilot is also called the captain. The copilot is also called the first officer. The copilot sits beside the pilot and helps during the trip by looking out for problems and talking to air traffic control. The pilot can ask the copilot to take over the flight controls.

Air traffic controllers Air traffic controllers speak to pilots by radio. They monitor aircraft safety by watching the weather conditions and all the planes around the airport.

Air marshaller At takeoff and landing, the pilot looks out for an air marshaller, who makes special hand and arm signals to guide a pilot in the right direction. The pilot knows what each signal means.

Cabin crew The crew of a plane makes sure the passengers are happy. They welcome passengers onto the plane, give safety talks, serve food and drinks, and help people off the plane at the end of the flight.

X-ray machine An X-ray machine takes a picture of the contents of a bag without opening it. The machine sends invisible X-rays through the bag instead. The X-rays pick out the shapes of items inside.

Passport A passport has the name and photo of a passenger, and the passenger's country and date of birth. You need a passport to travel from one country to another.

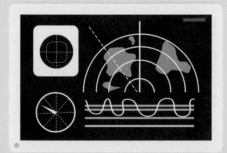

Radar This is an electronic machine that air traffic controllers and pilots use. On the plane, the radar can tell a pilot about the weather ahead of them. Pilots will try to avoid flying through bad weather. Pilots also use another type of electronic machine, called a TCAS. This lets them know when there are other planes flying nearby.

First American Edition 2016
Kane Miller, A Division of EDC Publishing

Copyright © 2016 The Ivy Press Limited

For information contact:
Kane Miller, A Division of EDC Publishing
PO Box 470663
Tulsa, OK 74147-0663
www.kanemiller.com
www.edcpub.com
www.usbornebooksandmore.com

Library of Congress Control Number: 2015938835

Printed in China

ISBN: 978-1-61067-412-6